The
Alexander Dobbin House
In Gettysburg
A Short History

Dr. Walter L. Powell

Ten Roads Publishing

Published by Ten Roads Publishing, LLC.
P.O. Box 3152
Gettysburg, Pennsylvana 17325

ISBN: 978-0-9837213-0-7

For more information on this title and others please visit our website at: **www.tenroadspublishing.com**

Or contact us via email at:

info@tenroadspublishing.com

Second Edition, 2011
**PRINTED AND BOUND IN
THE UNITED STATES OF AMERICA**

The Alexander Dobbin House in Gettysburg: A Short History

PREFACE

The history of the Alexander Dobbin House spans the life of the Gettysburg community, and in that time, many have lived or visited here who have left only the echoes of footprints behind. The hardest task for any historian is to find whether or not he has, as the poet Hart Crane noted, "fingers long enough to play old keys that are but echoes." While preparing the first printing of this work more than twenty years ago, and more recently, my task was made much easier by the kind assistance of many people, including Dr. Charles Glatfelter, Director Emeritus of the Adams County Historical Society in Gettysburg, and his enthusiastic successor, Wayne Motts, current Director; Tim Smith, author and Research Assistant at the Adams County Historical Society; Ben Neely, Curator at the Adams County Historical Society; Kathy Georg Harrison, Chief Historian at Gettysburg National Military Park; John Heiser, Historian, Gettysburg National Military Park; Mr. Michael Winey and Randy Hackenburg, formerly of the U.S. Army Military History Institute, Carlisle Barracks, Pennsylvania; the late Mary Snyder of Gettysburg; Mr. Alan Sessarego of Gettysburg; Mr. and Mrs. Robert Bishop of Gettysburg; Mrs. Pauline Adamik, former owner of the Dobbin House, and her daughter Terry; Mr. and Mrs. Galen Kline of Carlisle; Dr. Ronald F. Schultz of Waynesboro, Pennsylvania; Rev. Dr. Reid Stewart of New Kensington, Pennsylvania; Ms. Joyce Adgate, Curator of the Pennsylvania Room at the Centre County Library and Historical Museum in Bellefonte, Pennsylvania; Ms. Susan Hannegan of the Centre County Planning Office; and Henry Timman and Matt Burr of the Firelands Historical Society in Norwalk, Ohio. My good friends William A. Frassanito, Elwood Christ, and Mary Lou Schwartz all deserve special thanks for providing me helpful leads, and for their enthusiastic readiness to share their enviable knowledge of Gettysburg's history.

I am very much indebted to Merry Bush, who has formatted this manuscript and illustrations and prepared it for publication. A special thanks goes to Jackie White, owner of the Dobbin House, a dedicated and most worthy successor of the Rev. Alexander Dobbin, who first encouraged me to embark on this work more than twenty years ago, and to Jim Glessner and Eric Lindblade of Ten Roads Publishing, who have made possible its renewed publication. Finally, but not least, I wish to thank my wife Susan Kinsey Powell, who knows what I cannot tell, and whose constant support and patience during my research makes her a kindred spirit of Isabella Dobbin.

Dr. Walter Louis Powell
Gettysburg, Pennsylvania
September 2009

Introduction

Gettysburg's oldest house stands as a witness to the illustrious career of one of this town's greatest residents, and as a reminder of the more than two centuries of our "local habitation and a name." The Reverend Alexander Dobbin—farmer, minister, theologian, educator, community leader—was a true embodiment of the 18th century philosophical movement known as the "Enlightenment," which led men and women like Dobbin to seek our nation's independence. It seems appropriate then, that of all the houses that stood in Gettysburg in 1776, Dobbin's alone survives.

Though Dobbin's name will remain forever linked with his stone house, many others have considered it home since the last member of the Dobbin family left in 1825. This study will provide an extended look at the lives of the Rev. Dobbin and his family, then go forward to glimpse more briefly at other people and events that have shaped the house to the present.

Home is the riddle of the wise —
the booty of the dove.

- Emily Dickinson

Chapter I

Beginnings: A New Pastor and a New House

The Reverend Alexander Dobbin was born in Londonderry, Northern Ireland on 4 February 1742, the son of Scottish parents. We know few details of his childhood, but family tradition notes that the Dobbin household was a strongly religious one, and that John Dobbin, a "pious sailor," encouraged his son Alexander to prepare for a career as a Presbyterian minister. The young Dobbin studied at grammar schools in Londonderry, where he received classical training in Greek and Latin, the two languages deemed most necessary at the time for a well rounded education. At a time when free public education simply did not exist, and grammar schools charged fees, one can only guess that the Dobbins made a considerable sacrifice to see their son obtained a good education. He entered Glasgow University in 1764, but after graduation in 1768, chose to continue his theological studies in Glasgow and Edinburgh instead of entering the ministry immediately. Perhaps his decision was influenced by the vigorous intellectual climate existing in the two cities, for this was the time of the "Scottish Enlightenment," when Edinburgh was called the "Athens of the North," and writers of international reputation like economist Adam Smith and philosopher David Hume were lecturers there. The number of books in his library by Alexander Erskine and Hugh Blair suggest that he may have studied under these noted Scottish theologians; in any case, Dobbin received the finest education available to any young man of his day.

Dobbin completed his theological studies in 1771 and began preaching in Aghadowney, Londonderry County, though he was not yet ordained. Sometime that year he was approached by Mr. William Brown of Paxton,

Lancaster County, in the Colony of Pennsylvania, who represented the interests of the Reformed Presbyterian or "Covenanter" congregations west of the Susquehanna River. Brown was seeking additional pastors to relieve the burden of the Rev. John Cuthbertson (1718-1791), who had served as Pennsylvania's only Covenanter pastor since 1751. Dobbin thought about the offer for more than a year, but when he was assured of an adequate salary, he agreed to go. The Reformed Presbytery of Ireland licensed him on 6 July 1773, and ordained him on 20 August of that year at Conlig, County Down, to serve as a missionary to the Covenanters of Pennsylvania. Usually, Presbyterian pastors were not ordained by the Presbytery until they were "called" by a specific congregation, but in this case, Dobbin was ordained "sine titulo" (without title) to serve wherever he might be needed.

The summer of 1773, Dobbin's 31st year, was a milestone in his life. In the final weeks before leaving for America he married Isabella Gamble, a native of County Down—nearly ten years his junior. Nothing has come to light so far about her background or how long they courted before they were married. In late August the newlyweds, accompanied by the Rev. Matthew Lind (a colleague of Dobbin's who was also called as a Covenanter pastor) embarked for North America, joining more than 150,000 "Scots-Irish" who emigrated from Ulster to America in the decade before the American Revolution. As one of Dobbin's future students, the Rev. John McJimsey, noted 60 years later, Alexander was "licensed, ordained, married, and sailed for America—all in the short period of six weeks."

The Dobbins and Rev. Lind arrived in New Castle, Delaware on 13 December 1773, welcomed there by Rev. Cuthbertson. A month later they traveled to Rock Creek, just north of the future town of Gettysburg, where Alexander was welcomed by David Dunwoody, who offered the young couple temporary lodging at his home. Rev. Dobbin then assumed charge of the Rock Creek congregation, where Dunwoody served as an elder — then meeting in a log building somewhere near the present intersection of the Carlisle (Route 34) and Table Rock Roads. Two months later, on March 10th, Dobbin, Cuthbertson and Lind met at Paxton, Pennsylvania to establish the Reformed Presbytery of North America. At that first meeting of the new Presbytery, Dobbin was permanently assigned to the Rock Creek congregation, and on 24 May 1774, he was officially installed there with a "laying on of hands." He would serve that congregation for the rest of his life.

Like many other pastors in the 18th century, Dobbin probably obtained a guarantee from his future congregation to secure land and build him a house. The land on which his house would be built was owned by John Carson, who, with Samuel Gettys, claimed much of the land on which the Borough of Gettysburg is now located. Carson and Gettys were among approximately 150 heads of families who had moved into the area called the "Marsh Creek Settlement" by 1741. Though Carson did not sell to Dobbin until 1779, it is likely they had come to a property agreement beforehand, and construction of the stone manse appears to have begun in the spring of 1776. According to tradition, the work was done by David Dunwoody, a builder and stone mason, who constructed a Georgian vernacular style house that would have looked very much in place in Northern Ireland or Scotland — a two-story stone structure, five bays across and two rooms deep, with a medium pitched roof and paired end chimneys. At the south end of the house he constructed a one and a half story kitchen and springhouse, giving the building an overall dimension of 58 by 32 feet. The exposed fieldstone from which the walls of the house were constructed was probably covered with whitewash in the

18th century, for consistent with rural practice in much of Ireland and Scotland, the stone walls were pointed with lime mortar and harling, a rough cast with dry dash which concealed the stones behind a whitish surface. Late 19th century photographs of the house show evidence of this dry dash remaining.

The Dobbin House ca. 1913.
Image courtesy Adams County Historical Society

One anecdote about the house has come down during the period of its construction. While the building was underway, David Dunwoody, also a church elder, complained that some of the stones that had been quarried were not of the best quality. Hearing this, Dobbin replied: "You'll have to do with the stone as the congregation does in making elders— when the best material is all used up they have to used cobblestones!" According to the diary of Rev. Cuthbertson, the Dobbin House was consecrated at a meeting of the Reformed Presbytery in Gettysburg on 26 August 1776—just over a month after the Declaration of Independence had been signed in Philadelphia.

CHAPTER II

The Life Of A Country Pastor

Regrettably, no letters or portraits survive to give us a more complete picture of Alexander Dobbin, but we do know a great deal about his personality and his life as a pastor from reminiscences left by his son, Matthew, and several of his former students, including the Rev. John McJimsey, and Rev. James Mathews. From them we learn that Dobbin was rather small in stature, with a large pointed nose, and a "bright black eye." He dressed conservatively, continuing to wear breeches, knee stockings and a wig even after those fashions fell out of favor. He spoke with a thick Scots accent, but did so clearly, and had a rich, sonorous voice. Several anecdotes passed along by those who knew him indicate that he had seemingly boundless energy, an infectious smile, was slow to anger, and had a keen sense of humor. For example, on one occasion, when James Mathews accidentally drank from Dobbin's glass at a dinner party in Philadelphia, the good minister remarked: "I am glad to share with you in anything that will promote your enjoyment!" In another instance, while staying at overnight lodgings, the lady of the house asked how many children he had. He replied: Madam, I have seven sons, and every one of them has a sister." When the lady reacted with astonishment at the prospect that Dobbin had 14 children, he quickly advised her that he had seven sons, but only one daughter.

There is little question that Rev. Dobbin was a hard working man, as the legacy of his accomplishments attest. Forced to split his loyalties between family, church, and community, he was, first and foremost, a family man, for the 18th century Calvinist theologian in him was reminded that:

A family is the seminary of Church and State, and if Children be not well principled there, all miscarrieth . . . Families are societies that must be sanctified to God as well as Churches; and the governors of them have as truly a charge of souls that are therein, as pastors have of the churches.

Dobbin's family responsibilities would be considerable, for between 1774 and 1791 Isabella bore him ten children: Matthew (1774), James (1777), Alexander (1779), William (1781), Joseph (1783), Infant Daniel, died 1785, Daniel (1787), Mary, died in infancy in 1788, Mary (1790), and Isabella (1791).

Unfortunately, we have no sketch of Isabella Dobbin, but she must have been a patient, loyal, and industrious helpmate. As the woman of a pre-industrial rural home in 18th century Pennsylvania, she had to be a jack of all trades, equally adept at spinning, weaving, sewing, cooking, and farming. Though the Dobbins were not a wealthy family, they lived in very comfortable circumstances compared to others in their congregation, and as the tax and census records show, Isabella had at least one servant to assist her with domestic chores for most of her married life.

To support the Rev. Dobbin and his family, his parishioners allowed him a yearly salary of between fifty and seventy pounds (in English Sterling), and, after 1800, when the use of the dollar as the local medium of exchange became standard, about $300.00 annually. Though this would roughly translate into a salary of between $35,000-$40,000 a year, it was (as it is now) barely enough to manage expenses. Moreover, this amount did not reflect the actual amount he received "cash in hand," for the local economy lacked much hard currency and relied to a large extent on barter for goods or services. As a result, many in the congregation paid their share of the minister's "rate" in produce or labor. The help was certainly needed, for by 1793, Dobbin had nearly 300 acres of land, and though not all was cultivated, the task of raising corn, rye, oats, and wheat, along with managing sheep, pigs, goats, cows and other animals was more than his family could manage. Like many of his friends in the ministry, Dobbin was forced to seek other means to supplement his cash income. He accomplished this in part by opening a brickyard at the southern edge of his property on what is now called Cemetery Hill—directly adjacent to the future site of the Gettysburg National Cemetery. A more enduring venture to supplement his income, however, was his decision in 1788 to open a "Classical Academy" at the Manse.

We are fortunate to have some details of those years when Dobbin taught, including those passed down by several of his students, including the Rev. John McJimsey, a native of Carroll's Tract (near Fairfield) in Adams County, Pennsylvania, and Rev. Dr. John Hemphill, later pastor in Hopewell, South Carolina. McJimsey, who attended the academy from 1788-1790, noted in 1848 that "as there was no similar institution in the region, it [the Academy] soon came to be extensively known and patronized; and it proved in its results to be of incalculable benefit to many of the youth of that district." Dobbin's former scholar also added that the Reverend was "much distinguished for his attainments in classical learning, particularly Latin, Greek, and Hebrew," prompting a ministerial colleague to observe that Dobbin's extemporaneous analyses of one of the Psalms at a meeting of Presbytery illustrated his "profound acquaintance with the original language and rules of criticism."

Though we have nothing of the day to day details of Dobbin's teaching, it is evident that he mixed firm discipline with kindness and patience, for the Rev. Dr. John Hemphill remarked that "I do not recollect ever seeing his temper ruffled." Dr. Hemphill went on to note that Dobbin, throughout the whole course of his ministry and teaching career, took to heart the admonition of the apostle Paul to his son Timothy as recorded in 2 Timothy II, 23-25: "But foolish and unlearned questions avoid, knowing that they do gender strife; be gentle to all men, apt to teach, in meekness instructing those that oppose themselves, if God peradventure will give them repentance to the acknowledging the truth."

Dobbin's Academy appears to have continued until at least the fall of 1804, the last time a notice appeared in Gettysburg's only paper, the *Adams Centinel*:

> September 19, 1804
>
> The Students of the Rev. A. Dobbin, hereby solicit the Public to favour them with their attendance, at the Court House, in Gettysburg, onWed., the third day of October next, where they hope to entertain them with some short Discourses, on interesting and amusing subjects— To begin at half past 10 o'clock.

In the sixteen or so years that Dobbin held classes, he taught more than sixty students, many of who achieved later prominence. John McJimsey, after a brief time as a missionary in Kentucky, became the pastor of the Neelytown Church in Orange County, New York, and later, following the footsteps of his teacher, instructed at classical academies in Albany, Poughkeepsie, and Montgomery, New York. Robert Proudfit became a distinguished Professor of Languages at Union College in Schenectady, New York. Other graduates included William Orbison, iron entrepreneur and founder of Orbisonia in Huntington County, Pennsylvania, and the Rev. David McConaughy, President of Washington College (later Washington and Jefferson College) in Washington, Pennsylvania from 1832-1849.

Dobbin's interest in education is further illustrated by two other accomplishments. In 1786 he was elected a trustee of Dickinson College in Carlisle, and continued in that capacity for several years, serving as the chairman of what now might be called the curriculum committee. A glimpse of the course of study he recommended as a prerequisite for acceptance as an undergraduate provides a probable clue as to what his own students were taking: "The students . . . shall be taught Latin Grammar . . . Aesop's Fables, Erasmus . . . Select Propertius, Ovid's Metamorphosis, Caesar's Commentaries, Virgil [and] the Greek Testament." As a trustee, Dobbin also sought to raise funds for the school, and actively solicited donations from his colleagues and the wealthier members of his congregation. Several of his students went on for undergraduate work at Dickinson, including John McJimsey, David McConaughy, John Young (pastor in Greencastle, Pennsylvania), John Reed (later a judge in Carlisle), and Dobbin's own son Daniel, who had previously helped as a tutor in his father's Academy.

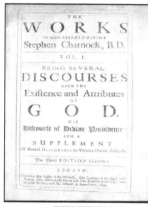

Title page of book owned by Rev. Dobbin with his autograph dated 1791 on the flyleaf. *Courtesy Adams County Historical Society.*

Portion of Dobbin's Estate Inventory listing books.
Courtesy Adams County Historical Society.

Beyond this achievement, Dobbin maintained a personal library of more than 300 volumes, the largest in Adams County during his lifetime. Because the titles he possessed were itemized for the estate inventory at his death in 1809, it is possible to get a sense of Alexander's wide ranging interests. As one might expect, many of the books dealt with Biblical criticism, such as *Brown on the Romans, Taylor on Titus, Frazer on Isaiah, Durham on Revelations, Commentary on the Epistle of John*, and *Discourses on the Book of Esther*. But he also had a considerable number of printed sermons, including the four volumes of *The Scotch Preacher: or a Collection of Sermons by Some of the Most Eminent Clergymen of the Church of Scotland* (Edinburgh: 1776), *Willison's Meditations*, and Alexander Erskine's *Works*. His collection of classical authors included works by Ovid, Juvenal, Terrence, Homer, Virgil, Sallust, Cicero and Xenophon. Rounding out the list were a variety of books on other subjects, including *Dilworth's Bookkeeping,*

Buchan's Domestic Medicine, Salmon's Geography, Farley's Defense of the Civil Magistrate and *Littleton's Dictionary.*

He was also a subscriber to several books published in Gettysburg by John Harper, including a two volume set of the sermons of the Rev. Hugh Blair. In all, this library was valued at more than $160.00—a substantial testimonial to the importance learning held for Alexander Dobbin. Regrettably, of all these books, only one appears to have survived to the present—Volume 1 of Stephen Charnock's *Several Discourses Upon the Existance and Attributes of God* (London: 1699), which bears the inscription "Rev. Alexander Dobbin in the year 1795"— now in the collections of the Adams County Historical Society.

Beyond his role as a family man and educator, Dobbin's most important responsibility was to his congregation. At first, he served only the Rock Creek charge, but he often provided services as a visiting pastor for other congregations. The diary of Rev. John Cuthbertson, along with the places listed in the record of marriages Dobbin performed from 1774-1808, indicates that in his first few years he traveled as far east as Lower Chanceford Township in York County (along the Susquehanna), and as far west as Redstone along the Monongahela River in Western Pennsylvania. In 1785, following the death of the Rev. John Murray, Dobbin also assumed the charge of the Associate Congregation of Marsh Creek—later known as the "Hill Church," and would thereafter serve the two congregations for the rest of his life.

As pastor, Alexander Dobbin was fully involved in the affairs of his churches. In addition to the many pastoral calls to homes, he had to spend considerable time preparing for the Sunday service, which would last all day. Unlike many others in the pulpit at this time, he did not prepare an entire written text beforehand in order to read his sermons, and certainly was quite the opposite of the Rev. Ezra Ripley of Concord, Massachusetts, who would write his sermons in longhand while standing, and would not quit until he was exhausted—convinced that the sermon was not long enough if his legs were not tired!

According to his son Matthew, "I never saw a sermon of his written out, though he could write very fast: but I had some hundreds of skeletons of sermons—merely the text and division into heads—from which he studied for the sake of order, and kept them before him to regulate his time in preaching." If Dobbin preferred to preach from simply an outline, his sermons were no less effective. According to Rev. Robert Proudfit, "as a preacher, his discourses were plain, solid, and instructive, destitute of all appearance of display," and Rev. John McJimsey recalled that "his method was to make a brief analysis of his subject, and, after mature reflection, to trust to his feelings in the delivery of the appropriate language." Furthermore, McJimsey added that "on Communion seasons he was especially appropriate and excellent," and it is no wonder, for the preparations for Communion (held only a few times a year) in the Reformed Presbyterian Church lasted from Wednesday through Sunday of the appointed week!

Though no sketches or descriptions have survived of the old Rock Creek church north of Gettysburg, there is much more information available on the "Hill Church" at Marsh Creek—not to be confused with the "Lower Marsh Creek" Church, another Presbyterian congregation, first organized in 1748, that continues to worship in the same building constructed at its current location on the Fairfield Road in 1790.

The Hill Church ca. 1890.
From the Dr. Walter L. Powell collection.

A log building was erected by the Associate Reformed body as early as 1763, and was replaced by the stone structure known as "Hill Church" in 1793. As the photographs included with this book suggest, the "meetinghouse" (as it was then called) was constructed in a conscious effort to avoid ostentation, in keeping with the Reformed Presbyterian's belief in emphasizing simplicity in the place of worship. Though the congregation merged with the congregation of Lower Marsh Creek Presbyterian Church in the late 1850s, the building continued to be used occasionally for worship services until it fell into ruins early in the 20th century.

A description of the interior provided by Francis Cunningham Harper in 1929 is especially useful, for while her childhood memories of the building were long after Dobbin's death, the interior had changed little but for the addition of a wood stove:

The "Hill Church" was much like the present Marsh Creek Presbyterian Church in architecture, but was a larger, somewhat more pretentious structure. It, too, was built of stone and had four doors of entrance. The aisles were brick paved and divided the interior into five blocks of pews. So high of back were the pews that when seated therein with the pew door closed, there was little temptation for the worshippers to gaze about them, for only the tall could see beyond the wooden box in which they sat. The ceiling was high and arched, and the paneled walnut pulpit was really a fine piece of workmanship. It had beautiful mouldings and delicate dentil ornamentation, and was embellished with a high sounding board. The minister's desk was reached by a steep, narrow winding stair, and immediately below was an enclosed stall for the precentor.

The "Hill Church" was not heated until after Dobbin's death, for as Mrs. Harper noted, her great-grandfather and other members felt that to "sit warmly and at ease while hearing the gospel was. . .a sinful pampering of the flesh." Moreover, no organ was ever installed, for unlike the Lutherans, Episcopalians, and Moravians, the Reformed Presbyterians opposed the use of musical instruments in the worship service. A Precentor used a tuning fork to set the pitch, then in his good bass or baritone voice, "lined out" a metrical paraphrase of one of the 150 Psalms, at the same time indicating which tune the congregation would use, such as "Dundee," "Old Hundreth," "Low Dutch" or "York."

Whatever the Rock Creek church looked like, by the first decade of the 19th century, the congregation there decided to build anew, and chose to relocate in the center of the town of Gettysburg. Construction of a new meetinghouse began in 1803 and was completed the following year using pledges provided by members to pay for the work. However, not all the subscribers were forthcoming in paying their pledges, forcing Trustees Hugh Dunwoody and Samuel Agnew to run the following notice in the Adams Centinel on January 16, 1805:

Fourteen months have elapsed since the last installment to the Church of the Rev. Alexander Dobbin, in Gettysburg, was due. The Trustees are bound for the payment of large sums, most of which are a considerable time due. Daily demands are making for money, and none to pay. They are therefore determined to prosecute, without exception, all delinquents after the 1st of February next. It is hoped this alternative will be prevented by punctual payments.

As a post Civil War photograph indicates, the meetinghouse (located on West High Street where the United Methodist Church now stands) resembled the "Hill Church" in its basic design, though brick was used rather than stone—brick very likely obtained from Dobbin's brickyard.

If Dobbin could take pride in the new meetinghouses built by his two growing congregations, he could take equal pride in the increasing demand for his participation in Presbytery and Synod affairs. As John McJimsey asserted: "Dobbin was remarkably punctual in his attendance of [these] meetings; and a full share of public duties, on these occasions, was always assigned to him." He was instrumental in effecting a merger of the Associate and Covenanter bodies, and his efforts led to the formation of the Associate Reformed Church on November 1, 1782. He regularly attended the meetings of the Associate Reformed Synod from 1782 until his death, though most of them alternated between Philadelphia and New York. In 1804 he served as Moderator for the First General Synod held in Greencastle, Pennsylvania, and the following year, he was asked to deliver the opening sermon at the Second General Synod in Philadelphia. His greatest honor was hosting the Fourth General Synod in Gettysburg on June 3-5, 1807, and he entertained delegates from New York, Pennsylvania, Kentucky and North Carolina.

Receipt for Robert Cunningham's payment of subscription to
"Gettistown Meetinghouse" signed by Alexander Dobbin.
From the Dr. Walter L. Powell collection.

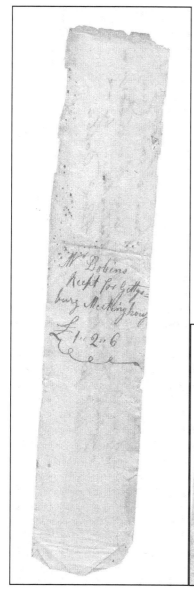

Interior of the Hill Church showing pulpit and sounding board ca. 1890.
From the Dr. Walter L. Powell collection.

With duties to family and church, it is hard to imagine that Rev. Dobbin found time for much else. Nevertheless, he did serve the community, and Adams County, in a number of capacities. During the first years of his ministry, before Gettysburg was founded, we have no record of what civic functions he might have served, though he certainly must have been active in supporting the Revolution from the pulpit, for the Scots- Irish Presbyterians were among the staunchest advocates of separation from Great Britain. Many in Dobbin's congregation did active military service in the Pennsylvania Line and in local militia companies, including John and David Agnew, John Dother (who served with Washington's Life Guard), John Knox, and John Edie. While the documentary record is not clear, Dobbin himself may have served in the militia. Following the War, Dobbin did become involved in the heated political question of whether the western part of York County should be separated to form a new one. One of the most prominent area settlers, James Gettys, laid out the future town of Gettysburg in 1786, and, hoping to promote settlement there, lobbied for the location as a possible county seat. In 1790, a commission of three men was appointed to investigate the issue of separation, but for some reason, was replaced the following year by another composed of Alexander Dobbin and David Moore. They were able to accomplish little until 1799, when, sensing strong support for Gettysburg, James Gettys deeded his 200 town lots along with the quit rents for them to Dobbin and Moore. Gettys also offered to assist in raising $7,000 to erect a new courthouse. On December 19, 1799, Dobbin presided at a meeting in Gettysburg to reach a decision on separation. He was clearly successful, for on January 22, 1800, the Pennsylvania Legislature authorized the creation of Adams County (after President John Adams). The following year, on February 25, 1801, Dobbin and Moore deeded title to the 200 lots to the new County Commissioners—Robert McIlhenny, Jacob Greenamire and David Edie.

With the county seat in Gettysburg, the town grew rapidly, and on March 10, 1806, the Legislature incorporated it as a borough. Because the original boundaries of the town were bordered at several places by Dobbin's land, the late Dr. Henry Stewart of Gettysburg noted in 1947 that the minister was "the 'deus ex machina' of the first addition to [Gettys'] original plan of Gettysburg—the extension from the lots fronting on the south side of High Street, over Baltimore Hill."

"Dobbin's Church" on West High Street in Gettysburg ca. 1870. *From the Dr. Walter L. Powell collection.*

The publication of those original boundaries by the Pennsylvania legislature is worth quoting completely:

> Beginning at the mouth of Culp's Run, and running in a straight line to the S.E. corner of Thomas Brandon's out-lot, thence in a straight line to the S.E. corner of lot No. 20 of Rev. Alexander Dobbin's small lots, thence to S.W. corner of the same, thence across the Emmittsburg road to the S.E. corner of said Rev. Alexander Dobbin's Spring lots, thence (so as to include said Spring lots) to the S.W. corner of William Buchanan's tan-yard lot, thence in a straight line to the S.E. corner of Newcomer and Hutchinson's out-lot, being No. 2 on plan of Alexander Cobean's out lots, thence along the different courses of the line between Rev. Alexander Dobbin's land and said out-lots, to a line of John Scott's land, thence by the outside lines of the said out-lots, to the Hagerstown Road, thence by lands of Alexander Boyd and others, along the line of Alexander Cobean's land, to the N.W. corner thereof, thence in a straight line to the junction of the Chambersburg and

Carlisle roads, thence to the mouth of Henry Weaver's Spring run, and from thence down Rock Creek to the place of beginning.

From this is becomes quite clear that Alexander Dobbin must share with James Gettys considerable credit in the establishment of Gettysburg. Not content to rest on his laurels, Dobbin joined in the subscription drive to build a new courthouse, and provided bricks, sand and stone to aid in its construction. He also served as treasurer of the Gettysburg and Petersburg Turnpike Commission, founded in 1807.

The last decade of Dobbin's life saw considerable changes at home, even while he was now established as a major figure in the church and community. On August 19, 1800, Isabella died. The cause of her death is unknown, and one can only imagine Alexander's grief at the loss of his wife of 27 years. He did not wait long to remarry, however, for less than a year later he joined hands with forty-five year old Mary Irwin Agnew, the widow of Ensign David Agnew, one of the wealthiest landowners in Adams County.

The Agnews had been members of the "Hill Church," and were close friends with the Dobbin family, so the transition for Mary to wife and stepmother was probably easier than might be expected. Though Mary brought a considerable legacy with her from David's estate, she also had ten children, which added a greater burden to Dobbin's already crowded household! Moreover, just a few months earlier, Lett, Dobbin's black indentured servant, gave birth to two daughters, Becky and Eliza. With perhaps as many as twenty people in the house at this time, the brick and frame addition to the south side of the house was probably begun shortly afterward. The roof of the existing one story kitchen was raised to two stories, and two rooms and a porch were added above it, giving the house its present appearance. In all likelihood Lett was given the room directly above the kitchen (where the museum is now located), separating her from the main house, but giving her direct access by narrow stairway to the kitchen and springhouse below.

At the same time Alexander's household was growing, three of his sons, James, William and Alexander, Jr., moved out of the Manse to set up businesses in the community. James had been assisting his father with the classical school, but in April 1801, at the age of twenty-four, he was admitted to the Bar in Adams County, and set up a private law practice in a house his father owned on East Middle Street. When the Borough of Gettysburg held its first municipal elections in 1806, James was elected to Borough Council. Alexander, Jr. seems to have been the more business oriented son, though less talented as a writer than his older brother, as his surviving letters illustrate. Perhaps with his father's financial aid, he and his younger brother William opened a dry goods store downtown in the spring of 1801. Over the next year, frequent ads appeared in the recently established newspaper the *Adams Centinel,* such as the following on November 23, 1802:

NEW GOODS
Just received from Philadelphia, and
now opening for SALE, by
ALEXR DOBBIN
In the Brick House, on the North side
of York Street, two doors west of
the Court-house
A FRESH SUPPLY OF
MERCHANDIZE
Of the latest importations, consisting of
DRY GOODS, of the newest fashions,
GROCERIES, HARDWARE, CUTLERY, etc.
Which he will sell, for Cash or Country
Produce, on such low terms as he trusts
will give general satisfaction to those
who will call on him.

The store did not succeed, and two years later, Alexander was running a series of ads in the *Adams Centinel* once again, this time notifying customers he was leaving the County, offering the store for rent, and asking his debtors to settle accounts. In the Spring of 1805, his father ran an ad offering the house and store for sale, suggesting that his son's debts may have been considerable. Indeed, debts contracted by Alexander, Jr. would trouble the family later, as I will note in the next chapter.

Just a year after Alexander, Jr. opened the store, his brother William died, followed in less than a month by Joseph, about whom nothing has survived. What killed the two young men in April and May of 1802 is not recorded, though it may well have been smallpox, for Dr. Samuel Agnew, Mary Agnew Dobbin's brother-in-law, recorded several cases that spring, and noted that he performed seventeen cowpox vaccinations. Shortly after Joseph's death, the Rev. Dobbin accompanied a colleague on a journey in York County, and years later, that companion wrote of Dobbin's reaction to the death of his sons: "In 1802 I traveled in company with him from Chanceford to Oxford. It was soon after a severe domestic affliction, in the death, I think, of two of his sons; and, I believe, I never witnessed a more striking example of Christian resignation—He spoke but little about his trials, but his whole deportment seemed to say, "The Lord gave and the Lord taketh away; blessed be the name of the Lord."

In the fall of 1808, Rev. Dobbin became ill. As his son Mathew later recalled: "In October, about the 20th, having caught a cold, and going to church in Gettysburg, he ruptured a blood vessel in his lungs by coughing, and was unable to preach any more." For the next several months, Dobbin struggled with what was very likely pulmonary tuberculosis, and died on June 1, 1809. Years later, one of Dobbin's students, the Rev. Dr. Samuel Knox, wrote of Rev. Dobbin's last hours:

> I have only the remaining impression, that during his decline his mind was tranquil. My father was his physician. I recollect, upon his returning home from his last visit to Mr. Dobbin, that he remarked with emotion, that upon entering his chamber, Mr. Dobbin looked up and put out his hand and said 'Well, doctor, you see that I am here yet, but the struggle will soon be over.' His mind and his conversation were then peaceful
> and cheerful.

A few days later, Rev. Dobbin's mortal remains were interred at Lower Marsh Creek cemetery, alongside his wife, Isabella, and sons William and Joseph. Perhaps no eulogy was more appropriate than that of Rev. Dr. Samuel Knox, who attended the funeral, and later remarked: "He lived and died respected and beloved and without reproach."

By the provisions of Alexander's will, written in December 1808, his eldest sons, Matthew and James were appointed executors of the estate. In addition to leaving his wife Mary the right to the furniture and other personal items she had brought with her when they married, he gave her "the remaining part of the time of my negro Servant—Lett, and one of my horse creatures . . . and two rooms which she shall choose, together with a privelege in the Kitchen and Springhouse in common with my son Matthew in the house . . ." The Manse and some 200 acres of farmland were left to Matthew, while James obtained a silver watch and "house and lot in Gettysburg." Alexander, Jr. received "Seventy five Acres of land on the western side of my Farm." The youngest children, Daniel, Isabella and Mary, all received cash—some to be paid them in installations by James and Matthew, and the rest to be raised from the sale of five lots. Of particular interest to Gettysburg residents today is the provision in Dobbin's will that "a twenty foot alley for the use of sundry out lots heretofore sold . . . should remain open forever for the use of the owners of said lots . . . said alley to extend in length from High Street to the western side of John Agnews and John Truxals lots." That alley, now known as Dobbin Alley, remains in use, and runs behind the house.

Tombstones of Rev. Alexander Dobbin and Isabella Dobbin
at Lower Marsh Creek Cemetery.

Chapter III

The Manse After Alexander: 1809-1863

The years following Alexander's death proved increasingly difficult for his family. Alexander, Jr., after a brief and unsuccessful venture in the business of hauling pig iron in Huntington County, returned to Gettysburg and renewed his efforts to sell dry goods. In November 1809 he joined in a partnership with Alexander Cobean, a prominent businessman and the founder of the Gettysburg National Bank in 1814. For unknown reasons, Dobbin and Cobean dissolved their partnership a few years later, and Alexander entered into another business with Thomas McKellip. In the spring of 1819, Cobean sued Dobbin to recover money due the estate of James Gettys, and Cobean won a judgment of $1,040. Despite his financial difficulties, Alexander, Jr. was held in high esteem by many of his fellow townsmen, being appointed to several Borough committees, and in May 1822, being elected as Burgess (Mayor). Tragically, he died just a few months later at the age of 43, with his debt to Cobean still unpaid.

James gained some prominence as a local politician, being elected to Gettysburg's first Borough Council in 1806, serving as Council clerk and treasurer, and from 1815-1817 being elected to three consecutive one year terms as Burgess. As an attorney, however, he was far less successful, for he had no business sense, and was, as historian Bradley Hoch has observed: "a very odd man, and just about everyone knew it." His friend Robert G. Harper, editor of the *Adams Sentinel*, writing some years after Dobbin's death, left a lengthy sketch of his friend that is worth quoting in part:

> I knew Mr. Dobbin from my childhood, and from that time on until his death I was almost the daily observer of his eccentricities. He had a singularly constituted mind. He was one of the best classical

scholars of the day. His father, the Rev. Dobbin, was the first teacher of the "languages" in this region, and was himself a very fine scholar. His son, James Dobbin, of whom we now speak, assisted his father in the school, and by this means became a splendid linguist, and so thorough was his familiarity with the classical writers, and so retentive was his memory, that at the last of his long life he would quote passage after passage, ad libitum, from Homer, Virgil, Horace, and others, and was the "book of reference" for us all in disputes upon such subjects . . . [He] was very learned in the law. He was always a student, and so powerful was his memory, that he rarely, if ever, forgot anything. For many years his brethren at the bar here would go to him when any abstruse point would present itself, and he would "help them out" by giving "day and date," "book and page." He was indeed extraordinary in this particular, and not only in the law, but in the history of the world and of the church . . . in short he was what you might term a walking encyclopedia . . . Yet with all this knowledge he was not a practical man, and could not apply it profitably to himself . . . To a stranger looking upon him from the street, he would appear to be a deranged man, for he was almost continually walking there, and making his speeches, in fancy, to the court and jury. He would throw his arms into every position, as though he was arguing a case, and sometimes in the most energetic and impassioned manner, completely absorbed by his subject, and unconscious of anything passing around him. He would go in and out of his office probably a hundred times a day; he could never be at rest. . .

On 6 August 1825 James lost his law library and a 200-acre farm in Franklin Township at Sheriff's Sale to Thaddeus Stevens, the rising young attorney and politician who moved to Gettysburg in 1816. The two men would face one another in many cases before the Court of Common Pleas in Adams County, and this action was a last straw for Dobbin, who, crippled by numerous debts, contended that Stevens was using his position as lawyer for the Bank of Gettysburg to effectively discourage other bidders and get his property for a fraction of its value. Dobbin sued Stevens, and a local jury, sympathetic to Dobbin, found Stevens guilty, but ultimately the Pennsylvania Supreme Court overturned the decision on appeal. According to Stevens's biographer Fawn Brodie, however, the younger lawyer was heckled for years at election rallies with cries of "Dobbin! Dobbin!" and "whether in fear for his reputation or in guilt for having wronged another," found a room for James, and later had him appointed as attorney for the Directors of the Poor, with rooms and an office at the County Almshouse north of town. James died at the Almshouse in 1852 at the age of seventy-five.

Dobbin's youngest son Daniel left the Manse while his father was still living, attending Dickinson College in Carlisle then going on to study medicine at the University of Pennsylvania. In 1807, the young physician moved to Bellefonte, Pennsylvania to establish a medical practice, and a few years later, married Eliza Harris, the daughter of James Harris, one of the founders of Bellefonte. The young couple made their home in a new two-story stone house presented by Eliza's father, and his practice flourished over the next several years. Wealth eluded Daniel, however, for, as one acquaintance noted later: "He kept no book to make charges, and, in consequence, at the end of a long and laborious practice, was poor. The rich and poor received his services alike." Dobbin died intestate on February 27, 1844 at the age of 58, leaving two young children, and forcing a sheriff's sale of his property to satisfy unpaid debts. His wife, Eliza had died three years earlier at the age of 47. As no stone had been placed on Daniel's grave, the residents of Bellefonte and vicinity raised funds a few years later to erect an obelisk which included in part the following tribute:

In his profession he stood high in the estimation of medical men, In consultation his opinion had much weight. In his practice he was very laborious and faithful. In his morals he was blameless.

Dr. Daniel Dobbin's grave.
Photo courtesy of Susan Hannegan.

Matthew continued to live at the Manse and work the estate, in company with his stepmother, two stepbrothers (Smith and Gibson Agnew), and his sisters Mary and Isabella. A few years later Isabella left the Manse, marrying local merchant John Edie, and giving birth to their only child, a daughter named Mary Dobbin Edie. After 14 years of marriage, however, Isabella sought a divorce—an action almost unheard of in early 19th century Pennsylvania. With the help of her brother James, she filed a petition with the Adams County Court on 25 August 1825—an action that may have been prompted in part by her husband's business failures and the fact that he was jailed for debt. He did not contest the divorce, and the Court granted her request on 27 January 1826. She later moved to Baltimore, dying there in 1844. Her daughter Mary never married, and died at the home of her cousin David Gamble near Emmitsburg, Maryland on July 15, 1847 at the age of 29. She is buried in the Gamble family plot at Tom's Creek Presbyterian Church.

Mary Dobbin lived on in her father's house until her death at age 30 on 14 April 1820. A poignant note in her will suggests how close she was to her family, for she requested "five pair of marble head & foot grave stones at Baltimore, at thirty dollars per pair" for her father, mother, two brothers and herself. That the graves were not marked previously no doubt reflected Rev. Alexander's belief that little ceremony should accompany the burial of the dead. The stones that Mary provided for her family still stand in the Lower Marsh Creek Presbyterian Cemetery.

When Alexander, Jr. died in 1822, the unpaid judgment against him was passed on to Matthew, apparently because the older brother had bought into the partnership of McKellip and Dobbin. Moreover, Matthew had contracted other debts; in January of that year the Bank of Gettysburg sued him to recover more than $2,200. For whatever reasons, Dobbin was faced with the loss of his father's house, and legal action to force a sale was apparently delayed only out of consideration for Mrs. Dobbin. Just a few months after her death on 31 August 1824, Matthew filed for bankruptcy, and on 20 April 1825 the Bank of Gettysburg purchased the Dobbin House at Sheriff's sale for $2300.

What Matthew did for the next several years is not known. By 1837, however, he had become a resident of Quincy, Pennsylvania in Franklin County, supporting himself as a teacher, and becoming very active in the anti-slavery movement as a "Conductor" on the "Underground Railroad." One of Matthew's followers, Hiram Wertz, recalled later his friend's zeal for the cause by telling of his reaction to the news that five black men had been arrested in Quincy:

> Hearing of this Mr. Dobbin rallied some of the citizens of the better class, saying that with them at his back he could demand the liberation of the fugitives. If the demand was not granted, then he proposed to use force. But the captors of the black men learned of the plan and hurried them away.

Matthew died in Quincy at the home of Hiram's father, David, in 1856. He was 82 years old, and the last of Alexander's children to survive.

Matthew A. Miller, ca. 1900. Miller moved to Tennessee and served in the Confederate Army.
Image courtesy William A. Frassanito

Matthew's activities in assisting fugitive slaves may be the reason why the Dobbin House has been identified traditionally as a "Station" on the "Underground Railroad." The tradition seems further reinforced by the presence of a sliding cupboard that conceals a closet-sized room located halfway up the narrow staircase between the kitchen and the "porch room" upstairs. Certainly Gettysburg was the scene of much Underground Railroad traffic, for as a crossroads community close to the Maryland border, the town shared with York the distinction of being what historian William H. Siebert identified "west of the Susquehanna River . . . [as] the stations chiefly sought by slaves escaping from the border counties of Maryland." As historian Margaret Creighton has noted, as early as 1841 members of Gettysburg's

African-American community formed a "Slave Refuge Society" and openly declared their intent to assist escaping slaves, and at least one African-American resident, Basil Biggs, is thought to have worked with his brother-in-law Edward Mathews, to aid fugitives at the small Black community of Yellow Hill (near present day Biglerville). Perhaps the local residents best known for aiding fugitive slaves were Thaddeus Stevens of Gettysburg and William Wright, a Quaker from York Springs. And there were certainly others. But as the Dobbin family was no longer associated with the house after 1825, and there is nothing to suggest that subsequent owners had any involvement in the anti-slavery movement, the claim that the house was an active "Station" on the Underground Railroad must remain a mystery.

While the Bank of Gettysburg acquired the Dobbin House at Sheriff's sale, a short time later Thomas Craig Miller (son of William Miller, the founder of Fairfield) purchased it from the Bank, and he owned it for the next 17 years. According to the author of an article written in the 10 May 1905 issue of the *Gettysburg Compiler*, "there are those who remember that General Thomas Craig Miller owned and occupied the home and also Samuel Witherow, a brother-in-law of General Miller." Miller, then serving as County Sheriff, was a veteran of the War of 1812, an officer in the state militia, and would eventually serve as a state senator. He lived in the house for several years, and there at least one of his sons, Matthew, was born in December 1830. In September 1842, General Miller transferred his title to the house to 36-year-old Conrad Snyder, a tavern keeper who operated the "Wagon Hotel" just a short distance from the Dobbin House at the junction of present Baltimore Street and Steinwehr Avenue. There is no evidence that Snyder and his family lived in the house at anytime, and it seems likely that this is when a long series of tenants began renting the building.

Snyder continued as the owner for the next 19 years; the house is listed in his name in both the 1850 and 1858 maps of Gettysburg. However, in June 1860, just five months before the election of Abraham Lincoln, Conrad died at the age of 54, leaving his widow Catherine and eleven children—seven under the age of fourteen! Mrs. Snyder sold the Dobbin House the following spring to James Pierce, a butcher whose home (which still stands) was located at the southwest corner of Baltimore and Breckenridge Streets in Gettysburg. Little could he realize that just two years later, his property would be caught in the middle of the most significant battle of the Civil War.

CHAPTER IV

The Dobbin House and The Battle Of Gettysburg

At the outset of the Civil War in April 1861, Gettysburg was a bustling crossroads community of some 2400 residents. The town was already known for its two growing institutions of higher learning—Pennsylvania College (now Gettysburg College), founded in 1832, and the Lutheran Theological Seminary, established in 1826. Moreover, Gettysburg was an important marketing center for area farmers, and had a reputation that extended beyond state lines for its carriage making trade.

The onset of hostilities brought mixed emotions in the town, for many area residents had family and business connections in the South. Nevertheless, some 3,000 men from throughout Adams County enlisted in militia units or the Union Army during the next four years. One of those recruits was John L. Ziegler, 34, of Company F, 87th Pennsylvania Volunteers— a unit mustered in York in September 1861, and composed largely of men from York and Adams Counties. John, a blacksmith, had moved to the Dobbin House in the spring of 1849 following his marriage to the former Alvira Cook. In the next ten years the young couple had five children—Anna, John, Elizabeth, Alice and Rufus. Ziegler's decision to enlist clearly reflected the pro-Union sentiments of a large number of Gettysburg citizens, for he had every good reason to stay at home. His youngest son Rufus was only two, and his wages as a blacksmith were likely at least as much as the thirteen dollars a month he could expect as a private.

Once John was in the army, it is likely he often sent letters home, but none so far have come to light. Alvira could also follow her husband's progress through frequent soldier letters published in the *Gettysburg Compiler*, including those of a soldier in the 87th Pennsylvania who used the pen name "Zoo Zoo." She shared in the frequent anxiety brought by rumors that Confederate troops were approaching town—the biggest on 9-10 October 1862, when a force of nearly 2,000 Confederate cavalry under General J.E.B. Stuart raided the nearby town of Chambersburg, less than 26 miles away. And, like many other women raising children while their husbands were away, she did her best to manage—a task not made any easier by the fact that for one period of seven months her hus band did not receive his pay. Expressing the anger and frustration of all of the men of the 87th Pennsylvania, "Zoo Zoo" wrote the following in a letter from Winchester, Virginia that appeared in the *Gettysburg Compiler* on March 28, 1863:

> The Paymasters are all dead, so far as we know, as we have seen none for several months . . . It is a fine thing for a man to love his country, and he certainly does love it when he is willing, for thirteen dollars a month, to sacrifice health, business prospects and everything, including his life perhaps, to uphold the old flag, but I tell you when a soldier knows that his little children are looking to their mother for something to eat and she has it not to give, and yet the Government owes him seven months' wages, if he growls, if he complains, nay, if for a few days he leaves his post to succor his little ones from starvation, who that has a heart will blame him? Let our soldiers be paid as promptly as those fat contractors who are fast becoming millionaires, and there will be no desertions and no suffering at home . . . A soldier's wife and children are as dear to him as are the offspring of those who are the upper crust of the land.

Earlier threats of a Confederate invasion became a harsh reality on 26 June 1863 when General Jubal Early's Division of General Richard Ewell's Second Army Corps marched into Gettysburg—advanced elements of Robert E. Lee's "Army of Northern Virginia." Though Early's men lingered only a few hours, the Confederate presence drew Union forces of the "Army of the Potomac" closer to a battle somewhere in central Pennsylvania. On the afternoon of 30 June, General John Buford's cavalry division rode to Gettysburg from nearby Emmitsburg, Maryland to screen Union troop movements from the south, and to reconnoiter for the main body of Lee's Army. The following morning, Buford's men clashed with the advancing infantry of General Johnston Pettigrew's North Carolina Brigade along Marsh Creek just west of town, thus firing the first shots of the Battle of Gettysburg.

The fighting of July 1, 1863 was west and north of town, and lasted about eight hours. With the bulk of General George Gordon Meade's 95,000 men of the Army of the Potomac still miles south of the town, some 16,000 Union soldiers attempted to delay a concentration of Lee's Army of 75,000 at the strategic crossroads here. Many of those men, divided between the First Corps of General John F. Reynolds and the Eleventh Corps of General Oliver Otis Howard, passed by the Dobbin House on the march to the battle that morning.

By late afternoon, both Union Corps were in full retreat, falling back through town to the high ground on Culp's Hill and Cemetery Hill — the latter position just a few hundred yards from the Dobbin House. At the lower end of Cemetery Hill, along the Taneytown Road, three regiments of Colonel Orland Smith's Brigade [55th Ohio, 73rd Ohio, 136th New York] of General Adolph Von Steinwehr's Division of the 11th Corps took position along a stonewall just a short distance from the Dobbin House. By nightfall, Lee's forces had captured Gettysburg, and the Dobbin House and barn suddenly became situated at the edge of a no man's land between the two lines. Many of the 16,000 Union and Confederate casualties that day were carried to the churches and other public buildings in town, including Dobbin's former church on West High Street.

On July 2 the fighting shifted to the south of town, opening about 3:30 P.M. with an attack by Confederate General James Longstreet's First Army Corps against the

Union left in the area of the Peach Orchard, Devil's Den and Little Round Top.

Grand Army of the Republic (GAR) Encampment on East Cemetery Hill, Summer 1880. Note Dobbin House at upper center, partly hidden by trees.

Image courtesy Adams County Historical Society.

Three hours later, Confederate General Richard Ewell's Second Corps attacked Union Twelfth Corps positions at Culp's Hill and Eleventh Corps positions at East Cemetery Hill. But at daybreak on July 2, long before this fighting took place, skirmishing broke out between sharpshooters positioned in buildings and behind manmade barriers at the edge of town, and as the day went on, substantial numbers of Confederate skirmishers were deployed between the Confederate main line on Seminary Ridge and Union positions near the Emmitsburg Road. Colonel Smith ordered skirmishers forward beyond the Emmitsburg

Road (now Steinwehr Avenue), and a detail of 12 men from the 55th Ohio took cover in Dobbin's old barn, just behind the Dobbin House. Here they discovered soldiers from the Union 1st Corps who had taken refuge here during the retreat the previous evening, including Corporal Simon Hubler of the 143rd Pennsylvania Regiment. Hubler later recalled "the Ohioans began shooting from apertures along the barn's heavy beams, and kept at it for more than an hour." When the Lieutenant in charge of the Ohioans asked for a volunteer to take a note back across the Emmitsburg Road to Colonel Charles Gambee, commander of the 55th Ohio, Hubler offered to go. After reaching the safety of the 55th Ohio's position some 200 yards away, and delivering the note, Hubler recalled:

> Evidently the note contained a request for more men because [Colonel Gambee] immediately detailed a squad of twelve more men, and inquired of me how they would find their way to the proper place. I told him that I was going to the barn because I had a wounded comrade there." At that point, in Hubler's words, "I told the detail to follow me and sprang over the wall, and running in a zig-zag fashion we all safely reached the barn.

While Union skirmishers took position in the Dobbin barn, at least one sharpshooter used the attic of the Dobbin House as a vantage point. Private James Carver of Company A, 55th Ohio exchanged fire with Confederate sharpshooters, eventually focusing his attention on what was likely the Jacob Stock House on South Washington Street [still standing at 430 South Washington Street]. There, according to Carver, "Rebels were firing from an upper window . . . the officer told me to dislodge them, but the window was at such an angle from me that I could not, and they threw a couple of shots . . . into the gable." The same unnamed Union officer then directed Carver to fire at a "brick house on the east and north of the house I was in, where a rebel had punched out a brick between two windows and picked off two or three of our men going through the orchard." In Carver's words "I must have done some execu tion, for the rebels sent a company of infantry over in the next lot under a grape arbor, and they fired two volleys into the house and I returned the fire. They then retreated with two wounded."

Where Alvira Ziegler and the children were at this time is unknown. As the house had no basement, it is likely they fled elsewhere. While her account of these critical days appears not to have survived, a number of Gettysburg civilians did write of their experiences, including John Rupp, a tanner whose home and business was just a short distance to the north of the Dobbin House at the corner of Baltimore Street and Steinwehr Avenue. Rupp wrote to his sister Anne in a letter on 19 July 1863:

> I hardly know where to begin to tell you our trials. When the Battle commenced on Wednesday morning we took our children and went over to Mr. [Solomon] Welty's Cellar. We stayed there until Wednesday evening. After the firing ceased, we came home and all slept on the floor that night, Such Sleep as it was. Thursday morning when the Battle again began we went to out own celler, and stayed there, that day. In the night of Thursday Father [Henry Rupp] came and took Caroline and the children up to his house. I was then in the celler by myself, that Thursday night, and all day Friday and Friday Night until Saturday morning, when Relief came by our Troops . . . If you could have heard the Shells fly over our house from Boath Sides—it was awful . . . I can't tell you all, it would take me a week to do so. Our house is pretty well Riddled—the Balls passing through our Bedsteads [though] no Shell Struck it . . .

Rupp mentioned damage to his home from musket fire, and likewise the Dobbin House suffered the same fate. Furthermore, the house was hit by artillery shells, for according to Private Carver "in about two or three hours the rebels threw four shells at the house; the first one struck the chimney on the east of the house, the second struck the northeast corner, the third struck about six feet from the ground on the north side, and the fourth near the west end, about ten feet from the ground."

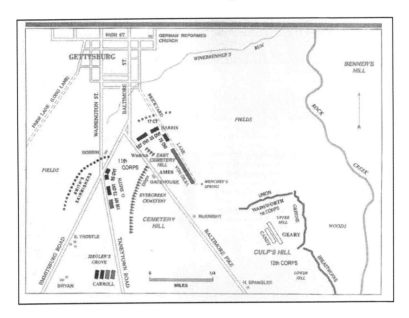

Map courtesy of Richard A. Baumgartner, author of *Buckeye Blood: Ohio at Gettysburg*.

Lt. Frederick H. Boalt, 55th Ohio Regiment.
Image courtesy of the Firelands Historical Society, Norwalk, Ohio.

Heavy skirmishing continued in the vicinity of the Dobbin House all day. At one point Company H of the 55th Ohio was driven from its position along a fence across Steinwehr Avenue, south of the Dobbin House. The house and barn also appear to have been recaptured by the Confederates. Responding to this renewed threat so close to his position, Colonel Gambee ordered Lieutenant Frederick H. Boalt of Company D to reinforce the skirmishers and retake the house. As Captain Hartwell Osborn later recalled:

> Volunteers were called for, and [Lieutenant] F.H. Boalt responded. He called for volunteers among the men of the regiment, and instantly secured as many as were needed. He did not take many, possibly twenty or twenty five, more would have attracted attention. With this little force crawling along the Taneytown Road leading into Gettysburg and keeping under cover as much as possible, he was discovered by the Rebel line of battle before the sharpshooters in the house grasped the situation. There was but one thing to do, namely to go ahead, and that he did. He made a rush for the house and captured it, and held it during the remainder of the battle; most of the men, however, were afterwards taken by the enemy.

Hartwell Osborn,
Captain Company B

Moses Pugh,
Sergeant, Company H

With the 55th Ohio in the attack on the Dobbin barn.

Among the casualties suffered by the 55th Ohio during action at the Dobbin House and barn were 11 men killed or mortally wounded, including 18 year old Haskell Farr of Norwalk, Ohio, who "suffered a compound fracture of the right thigh and wounded in the privates on 2nd July" and died on the 3rd of October at Camp Letterman—a field hospital established along the York Road just east of Gettysburg. Farr was later reburied in the National Cemetery, where he lies in grave E-6 of the Ohio plot.

Haskell Farr's grave and the Ohio plot marker
at Gettysburg National Cemetery.

The third day's fighting opened at Culp's Hill before sunrise, ending about eleven that morning, followed by a two hour lull. At one o'clock, some 140 Confederate cannon along Seminary Ridge (about one mile west of the Dobbin House) opened a two hour bombardment against the Union lines on Cemetery Hill and Cemetery Ridge to the south. The two hour cannonade was followed at three o'clock by perhaps the most famous infantry assault in American military history—popularly known as "Pickett's Charge." General Lee's grand stratagem to break the center of the Union line on Cemetery Ridge with some 12,000 men proved a bloody failure, effectively ending his hopes of winning a major victory on Northern soil, and forcing him to begin preparations to retreat to Virginia. The human cost had been immeasurable, but translated into cold statistics, of the approximately 170,000 men who fought here, 51,000 were killed or wounded.

55th Ohio Monument, corner of Taneytown Road and Steinwehr Avenue, dedicated September 14, 1887.

Image by Tipton and Myers of the Dobbin House (left center, behind
trees) from the National Cemetery, Summer 1869.
Image courtesy William A. Frassanito.

Though Alvira Ziegler and her children endured
one of the worst battles of the war, John was not in the
fighting here, for the 87th Pennsylvania was not attached
to the Army of the Potomac during the Campaign. Just two
weeks earlier, during Lee's initial advance down the
Shenandoah Valley, the 87th was part of General Robert
Milroy's command stationed at Winchester, Virginia, and
here they were involved in a stiff action with General
Richard S. Ewell's 2nd Corps of Lee's army. During the
battle, the 87th was forced to retreat, and a large part of the
regiment was captured. Alvira must have been very
relieved to learn a few days later that her husband was not
among those wounded or captured, for some of the men in
Company F came back to Gettysburg. As local resident
Sarah Broadhead noted in her diary on June 19:

> Another excitement to-day. The 87th Pennsylvania Volunteers
> is composed of men from this and adjacent counties, one company from

our town being of the number. Word came that the captain, both lieutenants, and nearly all the officers and men had been killed or captured. Such a time as we had with those having friends in the regiment! At 10 o'clock it was rumored that some of the men were coming in on the Chambersburg pike, and not long after about one dozen of those who lived in town came in, and their report and presence relieved some and agonized others . . .

Whether John was among those who returned remains a mystery. Among those Gettysburg men not so fortunate was Corporal Johnston Skelly, who was mortally wounded and died shortly thereafter. He was a close friend of Mary Virginia Wade, the only civilian in Gettysburg killed during the battle.

While John Ziegler did not fight at Gettysburg, other Gettysburg men were here. Assigned to General George Sykes Fifth Corps of the Army of the Potomac, the men from Company K of the First Pennsylvania Reserves, entirely recruited in Adams County, sustained a number of casualties in the "Wheatfield" fighting on July 2nd. Nine of the men in this company were from Gettysburg, including Captain Henry Minnigh, Lieutenant George Kitzmiller, and Sergeant Michael Murray Miller. Another member of this company, though wounded previously and not present during the battle was Jay Shaw Pierce, the son of Dobbin House owner James Pierce.

A few days after the battle, Hiram Wertz visited Gettysburg. Seeing the Dobbin House prompted memories of his friend and mentor Matthew, and recalling his thoughts on this occasion nearly fifty years later, he wrote:

. . . I stood on Cemetery hill, and, looking westward, the Dobbin homestead lay before me, the old stone house, in which the enthusiastic abolitionist had been born, defaced with shot and shell, with devastation all around it. It came upon me in an overwhelming manner that if Mr. Dobbin could have seen this and have known that there the backbone of slavery's defenders was broken he would have lifted up his voice and in fervent tones repeated the language of the prophet Simeon when the Christ Child was placed in his arms: 'Lord, now Lettest Thou Thy servant depart in peace.'

Grave of Hiram Wertz.
Quincy, Franklin County, Pennsylvania.

CHAPTER V

From Tenant House To Museum, 1863-1941

In the aftermath of the battle, a number of Gettysburg residents had to cope with major property damage. Some tried with little success to put in claims for damages to the state and federal governments, including James Pierce. Conrad Snyder's widow Catherine, still living at the Wagon Hotel, had suffered shell damage to her building, but according to her granddaughter, Margaret Gettle, she "never got any reparation payment for her damages [because] the man she talked to discouraged her from trying and she didn't know how to go about it further." However Alvira managed through this period one can only guess, but she must have been very glad to see her husband return the following fall! John L. Ziegler mustered out of the 87th Pennsylvania on 13 October 1864, having served as company cook. Within the next six years, he and his family left the Borough, for nothing more of them appears.

In July 1866 James Pierce sold the Dobbin House to John Rupp, a close neighbor who owned a tannery on Baltimore Street. Rupp held the property for only three years, selling it to Henry W. Heck in April 1869 — perhaps to help finance the recent construction of his splendid new "Gothic Cottage" [Still standing at 451 Baltimore Street]. Heck would keep title for the next 35 years, longer than anyone else but Rev. Dobbin. He seems to have been the first one to divide the house for the purpose of renting to more than one family, for a pattern of double and sometimes triple occupancy continued much of the time he was landlord. In 1870, Jessiah and Martha Sefton moved to the house from Thurmont, Maryland, and remained there for the next 10-15 years. Sefton, trained as a wagon maker, eventually ran a produce car from Gettysburg to

Baltimore, and later became a Battlefield Guide. He and his wife had eight children! Joining them in the house about the same time were two other couples—Frank and Maria Rosensteel and John and Margaret Beck. How long they continued here is not certain, but in an interesting coincidence, the two women (who were sisters-in-law) gave birth to daughters just three months apart—Jennie Rosensteel and Iva Beck.

By the fall of 1888, it is certain that the Seftons, Rosensteels, and Becks had moved elsewhere, for in that year, Rev. W. Melancthon Glasgow of Baltimore, visiting the house while preparing an article for the *Reformed Presbyterian and Covenanter* magazine, noted that the only resident was Mrs. Catherine Johns, the 58-year-old widow of Samuel Johns of Gettysburg (who had died in May 1887). Rev. Glasgow published his article in the October issue, and in addition to making a number of comments about the Rev. Dobbin and the history of the Reformed Presbyterians in the area, he provided the following description of the house:

> The building is remarkably well preserved for one in constant use for one hundred and twelve years . . . The interior is divided into spacious rooms, in which may yet be seen the woodenpegs in the walls, the traces of the shelves and bookcases in the "library" of Mr. Dobbin, and where the seats were in the "auditorium." Every room has an immense fireplace and a mantel as high as an ordinary person can reach. In some of the walls is made a large cavern, covered with iron, to keep out the dampness. Attached to the west end is a fireplace as large as a good sized room, enclosed by wooden doors, and would comfortably seat a halfdozen persons on a cold day . . . In one of the back window frames a hostile bullet is embedded, which was intended for a person appearing at the window during the battle of 1863. The west end outside wall is scarred by numerous bullets and some of the stones at the corners are broken by deadly balls and shells during the battle. At the very point of the outside gable wall on the east are yet plainly preserved the characters: "A.D. 1776." (pp. 350-51).

Mr. Henry Heck and Sophia Bosser Heck, ca. 1863.
Images provided courtesy of Mrs. Mary Snyder.

Postcard image of Dobbin House ca. 1905.
From the Dr. Walter L. Powell collection.

Rev. Glasgow's article, written not long after the 25th anniversary of the Battle of Gettysburg, must have prompted increased tourist interest in the structure, for within the next few years the first commercial photographs of the house were taken by William H. Tipton, best known locally as "The Battlefield Photographer." Early in the 20th century the Rotograph Company of New York produced a postcard showing the back of the house, and bearing the caption "The Old Dobbin School House, Gettysburg, Pa."

Mrs. Johns continued to live in the Dobbin House until her death in December 1906. She was remembered by her friend Emma Eckenrode (who moved into the house to help her in later years) as one: "held in high respect by many friends in this place for faithful service given them." It is not hard to imagine that some of that help went out to Mrs. Louisa Patterson Keckler, the 29 year old widow of William Keckler, who became another tenant with her three young children (Beulah, Ada and Grover) in the fall of 1895. Though Louisa could not have known it then, she would not remarry, and remained in the house for more than 40 years, leaving it shortly before her death in 1938. Her grandson, Mr. Robert Bishop of Gettysburg, spoke of her with deep emotion and pride, recalling that in spite of near poverty she successfully raised her children and helped put two of them through college.

In the course of Mrs. Keckler's long residence, the Dobbin House changed ownership three times. In April 1904, Henry Heck sold the building to William J. Collins. Just a year later, Collins transferred his title to Mrs. Kate Hay Nixon of Gettysburg. Mrs. Nixon's interest in the house was explained in an article in the 19 April 1905 issue of the *Gettysburg Compiler*:

> When the chapter of the D.A.R. was organized here about one year ago it occurred to Miss Jennie McCurdy, Regeant of the chapter, that a most laudable undertaking for the chapter would be to acquire the old Dobbin home . . . The idea met with great favor. Mrs. H.B. Nixon . . . purchased it last week for $1500 in order to give the local chapter the opportunity to buy it from her.

The *Compiler* article goes on to describe the Dobbin House at the time of Mrs. Nixon's purchase:

It is a colonial house. . .The front door swinging on hinges almost as long as the door is wide invites you in. There are twelve big rooms not counting the spring room. The wood work is largely oak. There are chair boards, mantles, old oak partitions, deep windows with small panes, doors on hinges handmade . . . Rafters are hewn logs. Some of the joists underneath the first floor have the bark on. There are unsealed ceilings, seven fire places running into the great stone chimneys flanking the house at either end.

For whatever reason, these plans fell through, and the property continued as a tenant house in Mrs. Nixon's hands until her death in August 1938.

Image of Dobbin House ca. 1928.
From the Dr. Walter L. Powell collection.

On 28 August 1940 John D. Lippy, Jr. of Gettysburg purchased the Dobbin House from Thomas Hay Nixon, Kate's son. A lifelong resident, John was well known as an entertainer and professional magician. He had a strong interest in American history, and enjoyed collecting books, documents, furniture, and other items of Americana. According to an article in the *Gettysburg Times* on 3 May 1941: "Mr. Lippy [had] long conceived a public use for [the house] as well as its preservation for many more years." After several months of preparation, in which he sought to furnish each room as it might have looked in Dobbin's day, he was ready to open the "Dobbin House Museum." On 15 May 1941 the following announcement appeared in the *Gettysburg Times*:

Three residents of Gettysburg, the only three surviving who are known to have been born in historic Dobbin house, Steinwehr Ave., now converted into a public museum, have been invited to attend the formal opening of the former classical school as a museum, Friday afternoon at 3 o'clock. John D. Lippy, Jr., who purchased the stone building some time ago and restored its interior, as near as possible, to its original state, announced that Brady Sefton, one of the three surviving residents known to have been born there, will sever a white ribbon and open the front door, officially opening the museum, at exercises Friday afternoon. Mrs. E.D. Hudson, formerly Miss Jennie Rosensteel, daughter of the late Frank J. and Maria Rosensteel, and Miss Iva Beck, daughter of the late John and Margaret Rosensteel Beck, have been invited to participate in the program. Mrs. Hudson and Miss Beck are first cousins. Their parents were residing in the Dobbin house when Mrs. Hudson and Miss Beck were born . . .

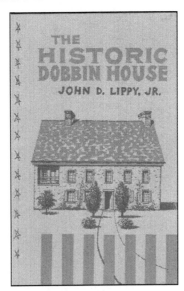

The opening of the Dobbin House Museum under Lippy's ownership began a chapter in the house's history that would last for thirteen years. A look at the way in which Lippy chose to restore the rooms in the house during this period not only reflected his interests, but the manner in which many house museums were being furnished in that period when the success of Colonial Williamsburg, Virginia (established in 1926) set a standard that many sought to imitate. *The Gettysburg Times* article for 3 May 1941 described the rooms:

All the rooms, with the exception of the rooms wherein are housed the old relics, are being retained in as near their original use as possible. Furnishings are originals or "exact" reproductions of the era of the late eighteenth century. Bedrooms and living rooms have been restored. One room has been set up as a school room. Within are old school benches and the "master's" desk, a hinged top affair. One room is a completely equipped spinning room. Here will be found a flax break, swift, reel, spinning wheel, wool wheel, spun flax and specimens of finished spun materials. Outside a flax seed bed is in growth. In the bedrooms will be found the old fashioned trundle beds, with hand-made coverlets, sheets, pillow cases, pillows and rugs. The large kitchen with its huge fireplace is equipped with old dough trays, hutch table, butter bowls, butter prints, flat irons, candle molds, skillets, snuff jars and other old kitchen utensils.

In those rooms set aside for the display of relics, Lippy presented quite a variety of items:

In the museum rooms will be found old newspapers dating back to 1797; Confederate money in denominations ranging from five cents to a $1,000 Bond; Civil war bayonets, holsters, buckles, bullet moulds, cartridge pouch, shells, powder flasks, haversacks, cavalry bits, metal epaulets, shrapnel time fuses, rifles, board axes . . . There are old apothecary utensils, quill pens, "Horn Books," old almanacs, hand made nails, locks, keys, knives, forks. There is a copy of the Rev. Mr. Dobbin's will; relics and photographs of Abraham Lincoln; a letter said to be in the handwriting of Mrs. Lincoln in which she had the official telegrapher of Washington advise President Lincoln that their son, Tad, had shown some improvement. This was the occasion of Lincoln's visit to Gettysburg when he dedicated the National Cemetery.

Less than a year after Lippy opened the Dobbin House Museum, America entered World War II, and tourism in Gettysburg came to a virtual standstill because of gas rationing and other wartime conservation measures. Once again the citizens of Gettysburg rallied to the challenge of supporting the country in time of need. Predicting that Americans would return to Gettysburg with the end of the War, Lippy opened another museum in August 1945—the "Lincoln Museum" in the David Wills House—where President Abraham Lincoln spent the night of November 18-19, 1863, and where he completed the final text of the Gettysburg Address. The 4 August 1945 issue of *The Gettysburg Times* noted:

Noon Saturday John D. Lippy, Jr. opened a Lincoln museum adjoining the Lincoln room on the second floor of the P.W. Stallsmith building, center square, the former Judge Wills residence, and placed on display a collection of Lincoln and Gettysburg connected articles of historical interest that Mr. Lippy has spent eight years gathering. The Lincoln room, facing on center square, is being restored to its 1863 appearance while the collection of Lincolniana has been placed on display in the large corner room, which for a number of years served as the law office of the late J.L. Williams, Esq. The museum is free and open to the public but a charge is made for admission to the Lincoln room.

CHAPTER VI

From Diorama to Restaurant

The Dobbin House continued under John D. Lippy, Jr.'s ownership until August 1954, when he sold it to "The Gettysburg Battlefield Diorama, Inc." This corporation, conceived by Curvin Heiss, Sr. of Gettysburg, was formed to exhibit more than 3,000 Civil War soldier miniatures which Heiss and his son "Corky" had completed. These were placed on a scale model of the Battlefield measuring eight feet wide and thirty-eight feet long—complete with flashing lights to simulate smoke, and a taped narration that included sound effects. In order to install the "Diorama," the inner walls on the second floor had to be removed to accommodate a small auditorium. A museum and gift shop continued downstairs. According to the promotional brochure created for this new attraction:

> The Gettysburg Battlefield Diorama shows you the highlights of the three days of Gettysburg in miniature with models scaled to the most exact detail and all figures are hand painted. Over six years in the making, the Diorama contains over 3,000 figures, 2,000 feet of wire, more than 450 electric bulbs, and is valued in excess of $25,000.

The "Diorama" became a well-known tourist destination, largely because it made one of the earliest uses of the new electronic technology of the 1950s that was capturing the imagination of Americans. Along with the "Electric Map" established at the Gettysburg National Museum by the Rosensteel family, it was a true forerunner of the many other sound and light attractions that would come to characterize Gettysburg's commercial district along Steinwehr Avenue. Then, too, Heiss was an innovator—one of the first "dioramists" in the post World War II era, and one who worked exclusively with 54 millimeter figures. As Gettysburg nativeand dioramist Michael Sheads has observed:

The intriguing aspect of his diorama was all of the ingenious handmade devices he created to make cannons smoke and rifle and cannon muzzles flash. Today, all of this would be done with servo and micro-electronics . . . but Curvin "imagineered" all the devices needed to make the action on the top of the platform come to life.

Curvin Heiss.
Image courtesy the Harrisburg Patriot – Sunday News.

In 1967 the "Gettysburg Battlefield Diorama, Inc." sold its rights and the house to John and Pauline Adamik of Aspers, Pennsylvania. The Adamiks worked hard to maintain the feature, including investing funds in the restoration of the Diorama. As Michael Sheads has recalled:

I was blessed with a commission to restore Curvin's original Gettysburg Battlefield Diorama at the Dobbin House in the early 1970's. The platform had deteriorated significantly as the result of several change of owners and pilferage. . . the restoration work was easily the most rewarding hobby related experience I ever enjoyed.

"Dobbin House ca. 1940"
Courtesy Gettysburg National Military Park.

Though the Adamiks worked enthusiastically to maintain the museum, increasing competition from other museums and attractions made it increasingly difficult to operate profitably, and in the summer of 1977, they sold the house to A. Kenneth and Thelma H. Dick of Gettysburg, though saving the "Diorama," which they dismantled in August of that year.

The purchase of the Dobbin House by Mr. and Mrs. Dick began a significant new and continuing chapter in the preservation of the building, and its popularity as a tourist attraction. Formerly the owners of "Fantasyland," a popular children's amusement park once located along the Taneytown Road just south of Gettysburg, the Dicks were moved to invest money in the building at the urging of their daughter, Jacqueline ("Jackie") White, who wished to see the building restored to its 18th century appearance and opened as a restaurant. Inspired by her many visits to Colonial Williamsburg, Jackie became convinced that a restaurant featuring an 18th century tavern and a menu of period "fare" would be the best economic means to maintain the house and keep it profitable. She also knew that such an undertaking would not be easy, for starting any new business requires a substantial investment, not to mention the fact that the house needed significant structural work.

"Dobbin House ca. 1967"
Image courtesy of the Adams County Historical Society.

Under the careful supervision of local contractors Don and Allen Crouse, the rehabilitation began in the fall of 1977, and almost immediately two challenges presented themselves—the need to raise the house eight inches (it had sunk after a main beam cracked), and to excavate a full basement under the building where only a crawlspace existed. The excavation was particularly challenging because spring water flows constantly underneath the house, and the soil to be removed could best be described as a quagmire of mud. The water had to be routed and contained, and the basement created deep enough to allow for its proposed commercial use as "The Springhouse Tavern."

In addition to these problems, the building needed entirely new electrical, plumbing, heating/air conditioning systems that would meet state codes for a commercial establishment, and yet be installed in such a way as to compromise the historic interior of the building as little as possible. Much of the original woodwork had been damaged or removed, and to restore it, Frank Auspitz of York was hired to repair or replace windows, shutters, fireplace mantles, chair rails and baseboards where needed. Some exterior changes were necessary to allow for a new kitchen addition, a fire escape and a doorway through an original wall to allow access to a restroom. Care was taken to construct these alterations so that they could be clearly distinguished as something new, and could be easily removed if a future owner wished to do so. The work was completed in the spring of 1978, and the "Dobbin House Restaurant" opened in May of that year.

The restoration of the Dobbin House was not only a testimony to the dedication of Jackie White and her family, but an important development in the growing movement to preserve and revitalize Gettysburg's historic buildings. On the eve of the Bicentennial of the American Revolution in 1975, prominent Gettysburg businessman Leroy Smith had restored the exterior of the David Wills House to its 1863 appearance, and a recently formed historic preservation group called "Historic Gettysburg-Adams County" had enlisted the help of President Dwight Eisenhower's widow Mamie Eisenhower to promote their efforts to raise funds to restore historic buildings. While Gettysburg's Borough Council had established a "Historic District" in 1972, many buildings of importance had already been demolished or significantly altered—creating growing concern among local residents.

Since 1978 Jackie White has assumed ownership of the Dobbin House and in August 1984 completed a major addition to the restaurant on the north side of the building.

Prior to beginning this construction in October 1983, Mrs. White permitted this writer the opportunity to undertake a salvage archaeological dig at the site. With some initial guidance from then Pennsylvania State Archaeologist Barry Kent, and Steven Warfel, and the field supervision of Stephen Hinks, then a graduate student in archaeology at the College of William and Mary in Williamsburg, Virginia, we excavated an area 18′x12′ to a depth of approximately 18 inches.

While we did not uncover any foundation features of earlier outbuildings, our excavation did reveal what was, in essence, a large trash midden that yielded more than 2,000 artifacts—ceramic and stoneware fragments, glass fragments, clay marbles, assorted nails, buttons, bottles—and relics of the battle—minie balls and shell fragments. Perhaps some of the most interesting finds were items that could well have come from the Dobbin household, including pieces of 18th century "Queensware" and "Chinese Export Porcelain." One other compelling find was a late 18th century stoneware chamber pot, reconstructed after locating widely scattered fragments. Since 18th century methods of disposing of garbage were less sanitary than our own, and because house holders literally threw trash "right out the window," it is entirely possible that someone in the Dobbin House tossed this pot out! The chamber pot, and other items discovered during this dig and during the restoration of the house are on exhibit in the "porch room" museum.

As the Dobbin House and the Borough of Gettysburg move forward into the 21st century, it is fascinating to speculate what it will look like 200 years from now. One thing is certain—as long as future owners share the same passion for history and dedication to preserving the house as those who have been its stewards, the legacy of Alexander Dobbin will remain secure. He would be pleased.

Bibliography

Primary Sources

Adams Centinel

Adams County Deed Books, Adams County Historical Society. Hereafter cited as ACHS.

Agnew, David. Estate Papers, ACHS.

Agnew, Samuel. "Smallpox." *Adams Centinel,* 18 April 1804.

Appearance and Judgment Dockets, 1819-1824. Prothonotary's Office, Adams County Courthouse.

The Christian Instructor. Volume I, No. IX, (May 1845); Volume 2, No. 1 (October 1845).

Cumberland Township Tax Lists, 1778-1828. ACHS.

Cuthbertson, John. "A Call Unto the Scattered Remnant of the True Covenanted Presbeterian Church of Christ . . ." Paxton, Pennsylvania, 8 February 1773. MS. Presbyterian Historical Society, Philadelphia.

Dickinson College Minutes. Volume I: 1783-1809. Dickinson College Archives, Carlisle, Pennsylvania.

Direct Tax of 1798. Microfilm, ACHS.

Dobbin, Alexander. Estate Papers, ACHS.

Dobbin, Alexander, Jr. Letters to William Orbison, Gettysburg, 1808- 1811. Orbison Family Papers, Pennsylvania State Archives, Harrisburg. Hereafter cited as PSA.

Dobbin, Alexander, Jr. Estate Papers, ACHS.

Dobbin, Daniel. Estate Papers. Copies at Centre County Historical Society, Bellefonte, Pennsylvania.

Dobbin, Daniel. Obituary in the *Centre Democrat,* Bellefonte, Pennsylvania, 2 March 1844.

Dobbin, Mary. Estate Papers, ACHS.

Extracts from the Minutes of the Proceedings of the First General Synod of the Associate-Reformed Church in North America; Held at Greencastle, Pa . . . 1804. New York: T&J Swords, 1804.

Extracts from the Minutes of the Proceedings of the Fourth General Synod . . . Held at Gettysburg . . . 1807. New York: Hopkins & Seymour, 1807.

Federal Claims (Civil War). Record Group 92, Volume 214. Microfilm,Gettysburg National Military Park. Hereafter cited as GNMP.

Financial Account Books, Old Hill Church (1798-1864), 2 volumes. PSA.

Gettle, Margaret to Dr. Charles H. Glatfelter, Lincoln, Nebraska, 16 February 1972. ACHS.

Gettysburg Compiler

Gettysburg Times

Proudfit, Robert to William Orbison, Schenectady, New York, 16 September 1839. Orbison Family Papers, PSA.

Receipt for Gettysburg Meetinghouse, 9 April 1804. From the Dr. Walter L. Powell collection, Gettysburg, Pennsylvania.

Records of the Associate Reformed Congregation of Gettysburg, 1808- 1810. Presbyterian Historical Society, Philadelphia.

Reed, John. "Copy of the Reminiscences written by Judge Reed for his children." Himes Papers, Dickinson College Archives, Carlisle, Pennsylvania.

Register of Negroes and Mulatto's, 1800-1818. Prothonotary's Office, Adams County Courthouse.

Rupp, John to Annie Rupp, Gettysburg, 19 July 1863. ACHS.

Sheriff's Deed Insolvent Debtors, Volume I. Prothonotary's Office, Adams County Courthouse.

Star & Sentinel.

Steward, Henry. "Rev. Alexander Dobbin—a Collation." Gettysburg, December 1947. ACHS.

United States Census, Adams County, 1800-1880. Microfilm, ACHS.

Secondary Sources

Baumgartner, Richard A. *Buckeye Blood: Ohio at Gettysburg.* Huntington,West Virginia: Blue Acorn Press, 2003

Brodie, Fawn. *Thaddeus Stevens: Scourge of the South.* New York: W.W.Norton, 1966

Busey, John W. *These Honored Dead: The Union Casualties at Gettysburg.* Hightstown, New Jersey: Longstreet House, 1988.

Centre County Historical Society, Bellefonte, Pennsylvania. Dr. Daniel Dobbin biographical sketch in the "Medicine Files."

Creighton, Margaret S. *The Colors of Courage: Gettysburg's Forgotten History — Immigrants, Women, and African Americans in the Civil War's Defining Battle.* New York: Basic Books, 2005.

Frassanito, William A. *Early Photography at Gettysburg.* Gettysburg, Pennsylvania: Thomas Publications, 1995.

Glasgow, W. Melancthon. *History of the Reformed Presbyterian Church in America.* Baltimore: Hill and Harvey, 1888.

Glasgow, W. M. "Covenanters at Gettysburg." *Reformed Presbyterian and Covenanter,* 26 (October 1888), 347-352.

Green, David. "A History of the Reformed Presbyterian Church in America to 1871." Dissertation. University of Pennsylvania, 1964.

Finley, Howard. *The Covenanter and the Frontier*. Detroit: 1937.

Harper, Francis Cunningham. "Reverend Alexander Dobbin and the Old Hill Church." *Gettysburg Compiler,* 9 November 1929.

History of Adams County, Pennsylvania. Chicago: Warner and Beers, 1886.

History of Franklin County, Pennsylvania. Chicago: Warner and Beers, 1887.

Hoch, Bradley R. *Thaddeus Stevens in Gettysburg: The Making of an Abolitionist*. Gettysburg, Pennsylvania: The Adams County Historical Society, 2005.

About the Author

Dr. Walter L. Powell is currently the Executive Director of the Conococheague Institute Museum and Library in Welsh Run, Franklin County, Pennsylvania, and Adjunct Professor of History at Mount Saint Mary's University in Emmitsburg, Maryland. He served previously for 17 years as Director of Planning and Historic Preservation for the Borough of Gettysburg where he directed the Borough's first Historic Building Survey, co-authored the Borough's Interpretive Plan (with Main Street-Gettysburg), directed the restoration of the Gettysburg Railroad Station (built 1858), and served as the Borough's liaison to the National Park Service Project Team that directed the restoration of the David Wills House (where President Lincoln completed the Gettysburg Address). The former President of the Association of Licensed Battlefield Guides and the Gettysburg Battlefield Preservation Association, he has written and lectured widely on Gettysburg's history. He lives on a portion of the Gettysburg Battlefield with his wife Susan and children Nat and Sally. He admits to sometimes wondering if he knew personally Rev. Alexander Dobbin and his family.

21239020R00038

Made in the USA
Lexington, KY
04 March 2013